WHO LIVED HERE?

My 1930s Home

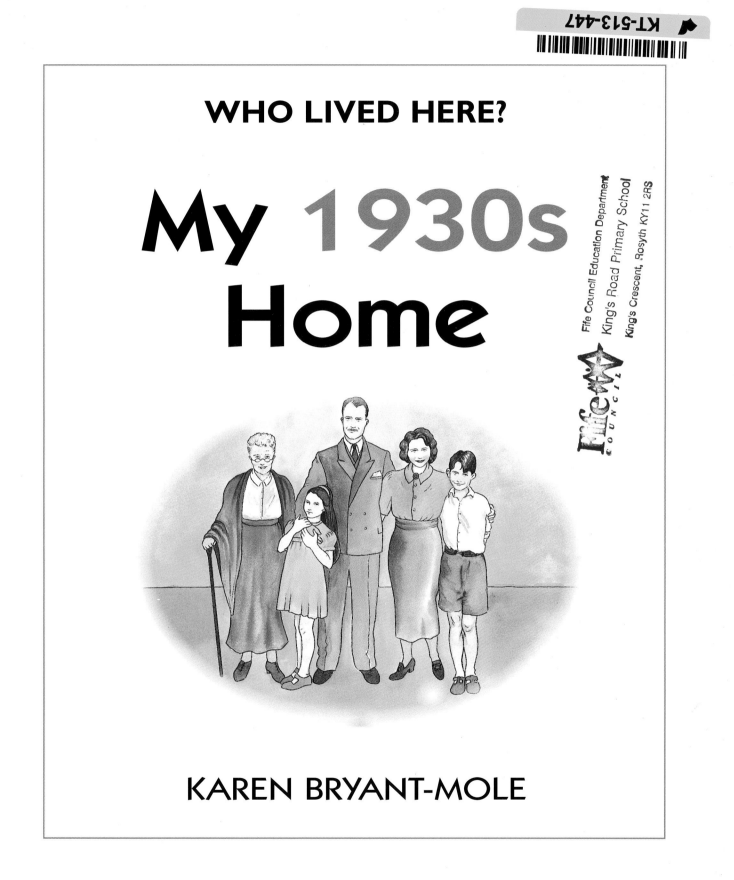

KAREN BRYANT-MOLE

FRANKLIN WATTS

LONDON • SYDNEY

This edition published in 2001 by

Franklin Watts
96 Leonard Street
London EC2A 4XD

Franklin Watts Australia
56 O'Riordan Street
Alexandria, Sydney
NSW 2015

ISBN 0 7496 4156 8

Dewey Decimal Classification Number 941.083

A CIP catalogue record for this book is available from the British Library.

10 9 8 7 6 5 4 3 2

Design and illustration: Chrissie Sloan
Photographer: Zul Mukhida

Consultant: Frank Jackson, Senior Lecturer
in History of Design, University of Brighton

Acknowledgements
The author and publisher would like to thank the Sunderjee family and the
Jungius family for their help in the production of this book.
Photographs: BT Archives 13 (bottom) and 30 (bottom); Beamish, The North of
England Open Air Museum 4 (both), 5 (both), 6 (top), 7 (top), 10, 15 (top),
21 (bottom), 25 (bottom), 27 (top), 29 (bottom); Chapel Studios 15
(bottom); Robert Opie 6 (bottom), 7 (bottom), 13 (top), 17 (both),
19 (both), 21 (top), 23 (both), 25 (top), 27 (bottom), 29 (top)

Printed in Malaysia

Contents

Some of the more difficult words are explained on page 31.

The 1930s

At the beginning of the 1930s, George V was king of Great Britain and Northern Ireland. He became king in 1910. George V was descended from a German family. When he became king, his family name was Saxe-Coburg-Gotha. In 1917, while Britain was at war with Germany, George V gave up all his German names and titles and announced that the royal house of Great Britain would be called the House of Windsor.

George V died in 1936. His elder son, Edward, should have been the next king. However, Edward wanted to marry a divorced woman. A king was not allowed to have a divorced woman as his wife and Edward was never crowned. Instead, his brother was crowned as George VI in 1937.

This is a picture of a street party that was held to celebrate Coronation Day.

The Depression

During the 1920s, America was a very rich country. But, in 1929, many companies suddenly went out of business. This led to terrible times for businesses all over the world. Millions of people were out of work. In England, the Depression affected the north much more than the south. The men in this picture walked from Jarrow to London, in 1936, to tell politicians and people in the south how difficult their lives were.

Entertainment

Life was very hard for many people in the early thirties. The cinema was an escape from this hardship. The first 'talking' film came out in 1928. Lots of glamorous Hollywood films were made during the thirties. Going to the cinema became one of the British people's favourite pastimes.

1930s Houses

During the Depression the price of goods in the shops fell. So, people who had jobs could actually buy more. Lots of people decided to buy houses. Millions of houses were built in the thirties. The homes shown here were in a cul-de-sac, or dead end road. Living in a cul-de-sac was quieter than living on a road that led somewhere.

SUPER **1933** HOMES

BARNEHURST PARK ESTATE
BARNEHURST, KENT

Estate Office : Station Approach, Barnehurst, Kent.
Telephone : Bexleyheath 406.

9'6 WEEKLY

£395 FREEHOLD

NEW IDEAL HOMESTEADS LTD
BRITAIN'S BIGGEST BUILDERS

Suburbs

Many people didn't want to live right in the middle of towns but they did want to live near towns. Living in suburbs became very popular. These were areas, on the outskirts of towns, that had houses and shops but very little industry. People used trains and buses to get to work. The houses in this picture were near a railway line that went up to London.

Council houses

In areas where lots of people were out of work, fewer people could afford new homes. Lots of people lived in very poor conditions, so local councils built new homes. Local councils are the organisations that run a town or area. Council houses were rented rather than bought. The tenants paid a weekly fee to the council for the use of the house.

Modern design

Most of the homes built during the thirties looked quite traditional. But some had a much more modern style. This house has curved walls and windows.

Glass was an important feature. There was glass in the front door. There was a window next to the door and more windows going up the staircase.

My Home

The house in this photograph was built in 1932. This is what it looks like today. There are lots of clues that tell us that it is a thirties house. The first clue is its style. It is built in a style called mock-Tudor.

Real Tudor homes were built between four and five hundred years ago. They had a framework of wooden beams. Although this house also has some wooden beams, they are just for decoration.

The chimney, too, has been built to look a bit like an old, Tudor chimney. In the thirties, the mock-Tudor house was one of the most popular types of home.

The large bay windows, that stick out in a box-shape, are typical of many thirties houses. Although the shape of the windows is the same as when the house was built, the windows themselves have been replaced with plastic-framed double glazing.

Other 1930s clues include the tile hanging on the bay between the upstairs and downstairs windows and the mixture of brickwork walls and pebbledashed walls. Pebbledash is a concrete mixture that contains small stones. It was used to cover plain brickwork.

Here are the family who now live in this house. They are called the Sunderjee family. Zul and Tess have one daughter, whose name is Leila. Leila is 10 years old. As you read through this book you will find out more about Leila, her family and their 1930s home.

The First Owners

This is the family who moved into the house when it was first built in 1932. They are called the Massey family. Mr and Mrs Massey had two children. Mary was 7 years old and Donald was 10. Mr Massey's mother also lived with them. Mr Massey had a good job in a bank, so the Massey family could afford to live quite well.

Mr and Mrs Massey knew each other when they were at school. They left school in 1910, when they were both fourteen, and got married in 1914, just before the start of the First World War. They spent most of the next four years apart. Mr Massey was in the army. Mrs Massey worked in a factory

making shells for cannons. Before the war, very few women had jobs. Now they kept both the war and the country going, as most of the men were away fighting. After the war ended, the Masseys were able to begin a proper married life together.

These drawing show you the plans of the upstairs and the downstairs of the Masseys' new house. You can look at the plans as you read the book. They will help you to work out where you are in the house.

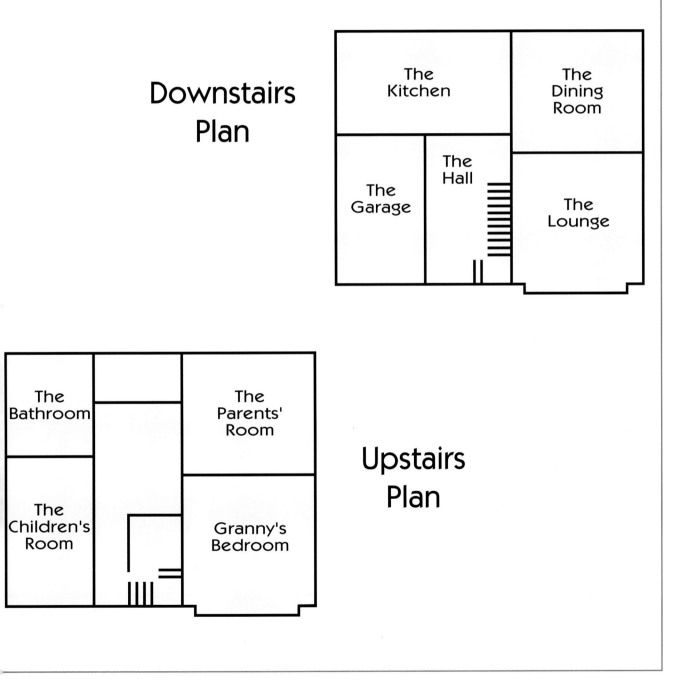

Downstairs
Plan

The Kitchen

The Dining Room

The Hall

The Garage

The Lounge

The Bathroom

The Parents' Room

The Children's Room

Granny's Bedroom

Upstairs
Plan

The Hall

This is what the hall looks like now. There is a telephone on a small table and a stool to sit on. Can you see the cupboard under the stairs?

This was the first room that a visitor would see. It was decorated in a way that made it look very grand.

The floor was covered in blocks of wood arranged in a pattern. This type of flooring is called parquet. There was a long narrow carpet down the middle of the hall.

This is how the hall looked when the Masseys moved into their brand new house.

The walls were covered in wood panels, as they still are today. Wood panelling was a very popular feature, especially in mock-Tudor homes. It was used to give the room an old-fashioned, banqueting hall look.

Between the stair rail and the stairs you can see some decorative wrought ironwork. The knob at the end of the stair rail is beautifully carved.

Electrical equipment

Mrs Massey kept a vacuum cleaner in the cupboard under the stairs. Electrical machines which helped the housewife with her work became widely available during the thirties. As well as showing a vacuum cleaner, this advert offers a range of electrical equipment, including an iron and a kettle.

Telephones

In the early thirties, some people had this type of telephone. It was the first phone with the listening and speaking parts in one handset. Before this, an earpiece was held in one hand and a mouthpiece in the other. It was still unusual to have a telephone. Even by the end of the thirties, fewer than a quarter of all households had a phone.

The Dining Room

The Sunderjees have fitted carpets in all the rooms in their house. Tess and Leila both play the piano. There is a painting of Leila's grandfather above the piano.

The walls were decorated in lightly-patterned, pale green wallpaper. During the 1920s two styles of decoration had been very popular. One used bright colours like orange, red or blue teamed with black. The other was to use black or dark brown together with white or cream. In the thirties, people started to prefer pastel colours, like pale pink, blue or green.

Like the hall, this room, too, had parquet flooring. There was a Chinese rug over the parquet floor. The dining table, chairs and sideboard all matched. The design of the furniture was quite plain and made from light-coloured wood.

The Masseys' tall, steel lamp was very fashionable. A fitted, gas fire heated the room.

Old and new

Not all families lived in new homes with new furnishings. The only way to tell that this photograph was taken in the 1930s is to look at the clothes the family were wearing.

Some families in the thirties were very large. There were fifteen children in this particular family!

Art Deco

This crockery was made in the Art Deco style. The name comes from an exhibition held in Paris in 1925, called 'Les Arts Decoratifs'. Art Deco designs often included geometric patterns and shapes. There was a jazzy look to the Art Deco style. Art Deco was very popular during the late twenties and through the thirties.

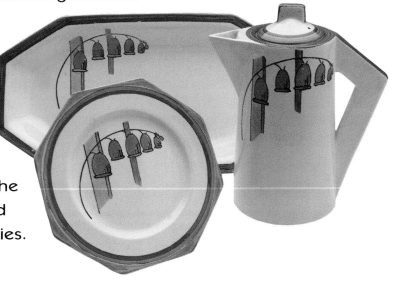

The Lounge

The Masseys had a radiogram for entertainment. You can see the radiogram underneath the small window. The lid of the large walnut cabinet opened to reveal a record player. It played a type of record known as a 78. They were called 78s because they turned 78 times a minute. Even though 78s were quite large they only played for about 5 minutes.

There was also a radio inside the radiogram. Very few families owned a television in the thirties. Instead, they listened to the radio. Mary and Donald loved listening to the special programmes for children.

The Masseys liked playing games together. Board games, like Monopoly, and card games, such as Pelmanism, became popular thirties games.

The Masseys had a mock-Tudor fireplace in their lounge. Although the fireplace is still there today, it is not often lit. Now, the house has central heating.

The Sunderjees have a television in their lounge. There are other televisions in the bedrooms, a stereo in the dining room and radios in the kitchen and bathroom.

Lloyd Loom

Many different styles of furniture were available during the 1930s. The Masseys lounge furniture was large and completely covered in material. But woven furniture was popular, too. The most famous make of woven furniture was Lloyd Loom. Lloyd Loom furniture usually had a diamond pattern on the back of its seats.

LLOYD LOOM WOVEN FIBRE FURNITURE OBTAINABLE IN ANY COLOUR

The National Grid

During the 1920s as the demand for electricity grew, the government set up the National Grid. This was a system for sending electricity all around the country. It was completed in 1933. Before electricity, homes had been lit by gas lights or oil lamps. By the end of the thirties most people had electric lighting in their homes.

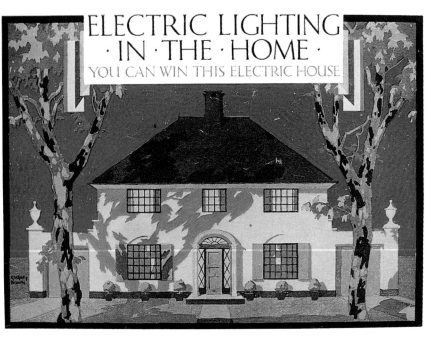

ELECTRIC LIGHTING · IN · THE · HOME · YOU CAN WIN THIS ELECTRIC HOUSE

The Kitchen

The Sunderjees' kitchen looks very streamlined. There is a long worksurface with an inset sink, a slot-in cooker and a built-under dishwasher.

There was a pine table in the middle of the room. Mrs Massey did all the mixing and chopping for her cooking on this table.

Mrs Massey kept her food cool in a cold cupboard, called a larder. One of her friends had a fridge. In the early thirties, fridges were very expensive and few families owned one. Most of the fridges that were available were American.

The kitchen looked very different when the Masseys first moved into this house. There was a stone sink, with a wooden draining board, and a cupboard underneath. Mrs Massey had a gas cooker. It had a small grill pan and a rack where plates could be warmed. Many 1930s cookers were painted in cream and green enamel paint.

Washing machines

A handle on the lid of this washing machine turned the paddle inside. After being washed, the clothes were put through two rollers on the back of the machine. These squeezed out the water. Although some people had a washing machine in the thirties, many well-off people sent their washing to a washerwoman or to a laundry.

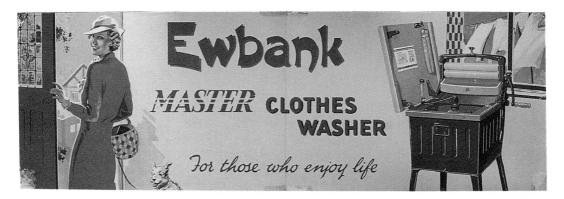

Kitchen equipment

Here are a few items that might have been found in a 1930s kitchen. Flour and bread were kept in enamelled storage bins. The black machine in the middle of the picture is a mincer. It was used to mince up raw or cooked meat. The machine on the right is an electric toaster!

Granny's Bedroom

This room was used by Mr Massey's mother. Mr Massey's father had died in 1931. Granny Massey had some savings in the bank. This meant she wasn't allowed a pension from the government. It wasn't until the 1940s that state pensions for all were introduced. Granny Massey got a small pension from the company her husband used to work for, but it wasn't enough to live on. So, when the Masseys moved into their new home they asked Granny Massey to live with them.

This is Tess and Zul's bedroom. The television and the bed are modern but the rest of the furniture in the room is antique. Some of the furniture is older than the house.

The Masseys gave their granny the biggest bedroom in the house, so that she could bring some of the furniture from her old house. Most of the furniture was about forty years old. It included a brass bed, a large wardrobe and a carved chair. Some of Granny Massey's belongings were modern. Can you spot her radio? It was a Christmas present from Mr and Mrs Massey.

Liners

Granny Massey had another son, who lived in America. In 1930, she and her husband travelled to America on board a huge passenger liner. Famous liners, like the Queen Mary and the Queen Elizabeth, were built during the thirties. Cruises on board these extravagent floating hotels were popular with rich people.

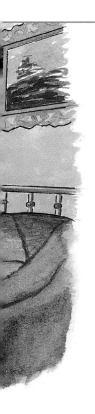

Holidays

Few people could afford expensive cruises. For most people, a summer holiday meant a week at the seaside in one of Britain's coastal resorts. Some people could not even afford that. It wasn't until 1938 that the Holidays with Pay Act gave workers a week's paid holiday. Before that, if people took a holiday, they usually lost their pay. Many people, like the families in this picture, made do with day trips.

The Bathroom

The Sunderjee family have a white bathroom suite with dark, wood fittings. The bath has a mixer tap with a shower fitment. Can you see some scales next to the bath?

The bathroom in this house had partly-tiled walls. There was a border of chequered tiles at the top of the tiling. The ceiling and the walls above the tiling were white-washed. The floor was covered in tiles made from linoleum, or lino, as it is more usually called today.

The Masseys' bathroom had a large, deep bath, a washbasin and a loo. The bath and washbasin were both plumbed in, which meant that water was piped directly to the taps. The taps were actually set into the bath and washbasin. Many people still had taps that hung over the bath or basin. In the 1930s it wasn't unusual to find people living in homes without any running water upstairs. These older homes usually had an outside loo, too.

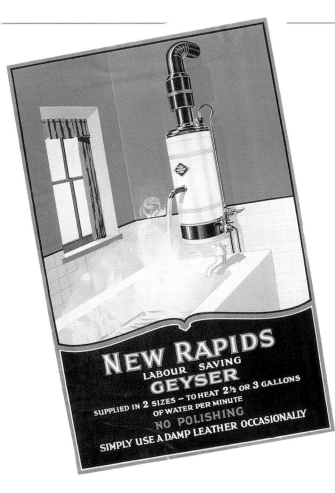

Hot water

The Masseys were lucky to have hot water that came straight to the taps. Many people used a geyser, like the one in this picture, to heat their bath water. As you can see, the water that came out of the geyser was often steaming hot. Instead of having two taps, this bath only has one.

Luxury bathrooms

Although in some homes there was no bathroom at all, in others the bathroom was the most luxurious room in the house. Look at this enormous bathroom. There was even a set of curtains that could be pulled around when the loo was in use!

The Parents' Bedroom

This was Mr and Mrs Massey's bedroom. If you look down at the photograph below, you will see that the Sunderjees still have a washbasin in the corner of their guest room.

Having washbasins in bedrooms was popular in the thirties. People were used to the idea of washing in their own bedrooms. Before houses had running water upstairs, each bedroom would have had a washstand with a jug and bowl.

This room is now used by the Sunderjees' guests. Their visitors have brought them gifts from all over the world.

The Masseys' bedroom furniture was quite large and chunky. It had a walnut veneer. This means that a thin layer of expensive walnut wood was glued over cheaper plywood. There was an eiderdown on the bed. The eiderdown was filled with duck feathers. Under the eiderdown were blankets and sheets.

Heating

The Sunderjees now have radiators in all the rooms. When the Masseys first moved into this house they had a coal fire in the lounge and a gas fire in the dining room but no heating at all upstairs. Portable heaters, that could be carried from one room to another, were often used to warm up a room. This is a picture of a portable oil heater.

Furniture

This picture of bedroom furniture was taken in 1936. Nowadays, a set of bedroom furniture is quite expensive and a vacuum cleaner or a fridge would be much cheaper. In the thirties it was the other way round. A bedroom suite would have cost about £18 but a vacuum cleaner could have cost £27 and a fridge was around £42!

The Children's Bedroom

Leila sleeps in this room. The puppet hanging on her chest of drawers comes from Sri Lanka. Can you see the tiny television on top of the chest of drawers?

Rugs covered varnished floorboards. Donald usually set up his clockwork train set on the floorboards. The train ran better on the boards than on a rug. Can you see the books on the bed? Mary liked 'Rupert Bear' annuals while Donald preferred Richmal Compton's 'Just William' books.

Mary and Donald shared a bedroom. They used their bedroom to play in as well as sleep in. Mary's favourite doll is sitting on top of the chest of drawers. She was a special type of doll, called a Shirley Temple doll. Shirley Temple was a child actress who appeared in a lot of films. During the thirties, millions of Shirley Temple dolls were sold.

School

Donald and Mary went to the same school. The children in this school are collecting their milk. From 1934, children in school were able to buy milk at a cheap rate. Children from poorer families were given free milk. During the forties, milk became free to all school children.

Toys

Toys that can be used for building things have always been very popular. The simplest building toys were wooden building bricks. This is a box of early Meccano. Meccano can still be bought today. Nowadays it is available with motors that make the models work.

The Garage

The Sunderjees have two cars. One is parked in the garage and the other is in the driveway.

The Masseys' house had a built-in garage but most houses that were built at this time would not have had a garage. Sometimes people bought their house before it was built. Many of these houses came with a range of optional extras. This meant that, for extra money, you could choose to have a garage.

The Masseys had an Austin car. They were very proud of it. Mr Massey and Donald washed it and polished it every Saturday. The Masseys used their car to visit relatives and they loved to go for picnics in the country.

Having a car was still quite unusual. Only a few of the Masseys' friends owned a car. Most people used trams, buses or trains to get to work and they did their shopping in local shops.

Factories

When cars were first made they were so expensive to produce that only rich people could afford them. Once they could be made in factories, the price started to fall. The car industry grew. This car is a Morris Cowley. It was made by the Morris car company in their Cowley works near Oxford.

Empty roads

This photograph of a main road was taken in 1931. There were only two cars parked there and people were walking in the middle of the road. Nowadays, there would be lots of parked cars and a steady stream of traffic. No-one today would choose to walk along the middle of a main road!

Elmfield Road, Gosforth. 8980

Things to Do

Suburbs

Many suburbs started off as small villages in the 1930s but have since grown into towns. Look at some thirties maps and compare them with today's maps. You may be able to see some 1930s maps in your local authority's planning department or in the reference section of your local library. Look for railway lines that lead into major towns. You will probably find that much of the development has been in places that have a railway station.

Telephones

Today, your telephone number has a dialling code for your area as well as your own phone number. Many dialling codes go back to the time when there were both letters and numbers on a dial. For instance, Brighton phone numbers start 0127. If you look at this phone you will see that the first two letters of Brighton, B and R, are above number 2 and number 7. Blackpool numbers start 0125, for B and L. Think of some other towns and use the phone book to check the numbers.

Plans

The plans on page 11, show you the layout of the Masseys' house. You could draw a plan of your home. Compare it with the Masseys' home. 1930s homes often had large halls. Does your home have a hall this size? The Masseys' house had a built-in garage. Where do people in your street park their cars?

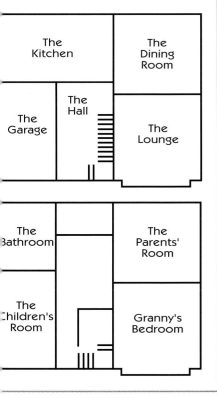

Glossary

Art Deco	a jazzy style that was popular in the 1920s and 1930s
banqueting hall	a large room where feasts were held
chequered	having a checked pattern
crockery	pottery bowls, plates, cups etc.
cruise	a holiday on a ship
double glazing	windows with two layers of glass
eiderdown	a thick cover, filled with duck feathers, that goes on a bed
enamel	a type of paint that does not crack when it gets hot
First World War	a war that took place in Europe between 1914 and 1918
geometric	using mathematical lines and shapes
geyser	a water heater
handset	a piece of equipment that is held in the hand
industry	business
liner	a large ship that belongs to a 'line' of passenger ships
mock-Tudor	in a style that looks like Tudor
optional	can choose whether or not to have something
parquet	wooden flooring made from pieces of wood arranged in a pattern
pension	money paid to someone after he or she retires
portable	can be carried
radiogram	a radio and record player (or gramophone) in one unit
streamlined	having flowing lines without breaks
suburbs	living areas around a town or city
traditional	in a style that has been used before
varnished	painted with a liquid that gives a shiny, see-through surface
washstand	a small table on which a jug and bowl were placed
wrought ironwork	iron bars that have been bent into a pattern

Index